The A to Z's for
Teaching Overseas
Teach Where You Travel

Written by Shanna Mack and Greg Parry

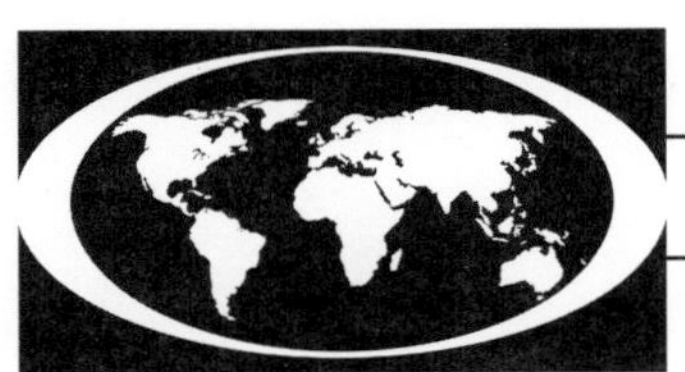

Published by Global Services in Education, Ltd.
For information contact info@GlobalServicesInEducation.com
Printed in China by Gold Printing Group, Ltd.

Edited by: Susan Cushing
Cover Design: Ed Davis
Special Thanks: Calie Torgerson

Photos: All photos sourced from www.shutterstock.com unless otherwise indicated.

The authors have chosen to use American English standards and conventions for this international publication.

ISBN: 978-0-9848185-1-8

Global Services in Education, Ltd. books are available at special quantity discounts to use as premiums and sales promotions or use in corporate training and induction programs. To contact a representative, please email us at publishing@GlobalServicesInEducation.com or visit our website www.GlobalServicesInEducation.com.

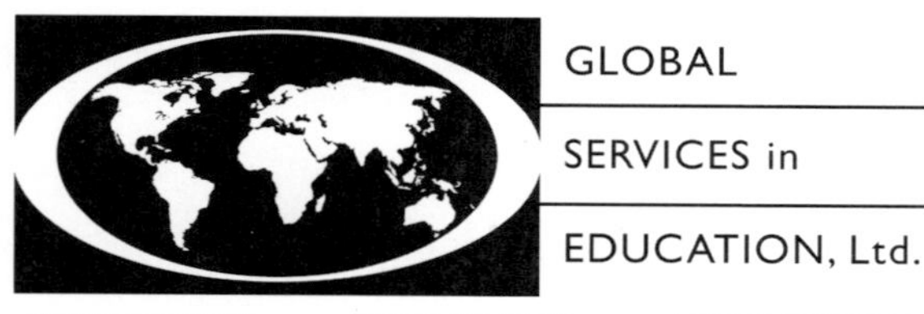

We would like to dedicate this book to our parents:
Bobby Joe and Marian Gay Gilbert

and

Wesley John and Beverley Elizabeth Parry

Through their demonstrated courage, strength and positive attitudes, they have inspired us to chase our dreams and see the world through open eyes.

We were once where you are now.

There was a time when we felt quite satisfied with the many accomplishments in our careers. Each day was as unpredictable as any other educator's day but we were moving along a traditional and steady path. Wistfully we dreamed of our future retirement which held the faraway promise of travel and exciting new experiences. But that was down the road...*later* in life.

Then, we woke up!

Re-evaluating our career and life plans reminded us that dreams are only realized when steps are taken towards them and it was time to take a new, exciting step. Why wait until retirement to travel the world and have enriching, life changing experiences?

We craved new challenges and new opportunities! It didn't make sense to wait!

When we first heard about teaching internationally, it was with tantalizing tales of:

- Exciting travel

- Complex and fulfilling professional challenges

- Rich cultural experiences

- Greater savings and financial opportunities

As firm believers in the old adage, "If it sounds too good to be true..." we were skeptical yet couldn't help but be intrigued. It took significant time and effort, but ultimately our careful and thorough research rendered amazing results.

Not only did we discover that what seemed "too good to be true" was in fact the *reality of international teaching,* but more importantly, it's a world that is within closer reach than most people would ever guess! Hopefully, this book will bring it even closer for you.

Educators can work in literally any region of the world, including some of the most amazing, unique and interesting locales. As international educators we have lived in and visited places that most would only dream of. We have climbed the Great Wall of China, shopped for our fresh vegetables at quaint, neighborhood markets and experienced local traditions, celebrations and festivals through the eyes of indigenous people who have welcomed us into their homes.

We will never forget our first days in China and how we delighted in the cultural differences we had never expected. Whether it was traveling in a taxi, bartering for

goods, eating strange foods or trying to pronounce difficult words, we learned that differences are exciting, fun and worth celebrating. Our lives have been changed forever with new perspectives and a way to see the world that is best labeled "global" but difficult to explain in short sentences. We love our own countries and visit family and friends often, but we equally love the people, travel destinations and cultures of other regions. We have experienced the world with a renewed perspective, appreciation and understanding. Our international experiences have also opened a whole new world of travel for family and friends, visiting us in locations they too only dreamt about.

The international teaching environment attracts professionals of all ages. We have worked with graduates and interns as well as retired professionals who decided to enhance their careers with new, challenging and different experiences. They enjoy the opportunity to educate children in different contexts with great resources, few behavior challenges and in a place they feel truly valued.

The lunch time conversations in international schools are very different to home:

> "Now that grades are in, I desperately need a break. I am heading to Sri Lanka for a couple of weeks. Two weeks on a beach, reading a book and eating amazing food!"

> "With a 10-week summer break I am torn whether to go home and see my family or travel around Europe for a couple of months."

> "I just bought a new camera for my safari in Nairobi! It has been a lifetime dream of mine to be up close to lions. I can't wait!"

> "I am trekking in Nepal this year then taking my history class next year. Now that is the kind of research I like to employ!"

While the financial opportunities clearly vary between regions, they are usually an added bonus to the lifestyle and opportunities international educators share. Higher salaries, housing included in employment, lower costs of living, full medical coverage, annual airfares home, no tax and many more benefits ensure savings grow at a far greater rate than our jobs did at home. It is nice to enjoy lifestyle opportunities that are now within our reach both geographically and financially. Although money was not our primary motivator for working overseas, it provided opportunities and choices that employment in our home countries did not.

We have experienced firsthand, both the highlights and the "red flags" of teaching overseas and we want others to benefit from these experiences. If you allow us, we can

guide you through the decision-making processes, challenges, transitions and exciting new opportunities so that you too can enjoy international education as much as we do. We hope this book underscores that you are not alone in this process and helps you to embrace the amazing opportunities that await.

We were once where you are now. It's an exciting adventure and we're here to help you each step of the way.

Greg and Shanna

Joint Founders and Lead Consultants - Global Services in Education, Ltd.

-A-

Accommodations: As a teacher working in an expatriate environment, you will have the advantages of living in a close-knit community with a great deal of support. Some schools may offer you your own apartment while at other schools you might share accommodations with other teachers.

Questions to ask regarding school-provided accommodations:
- Will all of my housing costs be covered?
- Will I have my own apartment?
- Will all of my utilities be covered?
- What do utilities include?
- Is a telephone included or easily accessible?
- Can you describe the security of the accommodations and of the surrounding area?
- Is internet included or easily accessible?
- Are there any additional management fees?
- Is cable/satellite TV provided?
- What standard furniture and appliances are included?
- Do I need to provide my own bedding, crockery, linen, etc.?
- Are cleaning/maid services available?
- Will I be living close to the school?
- Am I close to a shopping center?
- Is public transportation (bus, taxi, subway) easily accessible?
- Is there a gym, fitness center or recreational facility nearby?

In some international schools you may live on campus as part of the boarding facility.

Questions to ask regarding boarding school accommodations:
- Will I be required to perform extra duties? How often? What does a typical schedule look like?
- Do I have a private room?
- Do I have a private bathroom?
- Do I have access to a kitchen? If so, will there be a private area for me to store food?
- Is there a shared or private space for teachers to connect and socialize?
- Will all of my utilities be covered?

- What do utilities include?
- Is a telephone included or easily accessible?
- Can you describe the security of the accommodations and of the nearby area?
- Is internet included or easily accessible?
- Is cable/satellite TV provided?
- What standard furniture and appliances are included?
- Do I need to provide my own bedding, crockery, linen, etc.?
- Are cleaning/maid services available?
- Am I close to a shopping center?
- Is public transportation (bus, taxi, subway) easily accessible?
- Is there a gym, fitness center or recreational facility nearby?

Before accepting a position, make sure that you are comfortable with the living accommodations.

GREAT IDEA: Make it a daily practice to walk (or travel) to a new area of your neighborhood. The faster you feel comfortable in your local environment, the more at home you will be.

Adapting: You will meet teachers from all parts of the world with different levels of international experience. Draw on the experiences of colleagues but also connect with people outside of your school. Expatriate networks in your host country will be invaluable both as a resource and for new social connections. By expanding your networks you will broaden your experiences and meet exciting people from different walks of life.

While in your host country, use the opportunity to explore, see new sights and meet new people! We suggest frequenting spots where locals spend their time. Embrace the local cultures and traditions. You are living a once in a lifetime opportunity, make the most of it.

GREAT IDEA: Travel with something that represents home. Let this be one of the first things you unpack as you settle into your new home.

Admissions Process: Most international schools will have a thorough admissions process that includes an entrance exam for students. This process is usually led by the admissions department of the school. Typically, these tests will include English, reading comprehension, mathematics and a personal statement. It is also common for students

to submit previous academic reports, letters of recommendation and complete an oral interview.

Adoption Overseas: Adoption can be a complicated process requiring a great deal of research. It is important to explore the requirements for both your country of origin and the host country. For further information work through a reputable adoption agency.

Age Restrictions: Schools are looking for energetic, vibrant, high-quality teachers that match the needs of the students at their school. For most schools age will not be a factor in their selection process; however, some countries may have visa restrictions based on age. If this is your situation, don't be discouraged. There will be a region that matches your profile.

Alcohol Consumption: Different regions have different laws about the consumption of alcohol in public. In the Middle East, for example, you need a local license to purchase alcohol. As an international educator, you should have complete knowledge and respect for all laws in your host country.

Application Process: The best way to avoid confusion or delays is to utilize the services of a reputable international recruiting company. They can assist you with the application process as well as offer advice on various aspects relevant to the specific country where you are applying.

There are things you can do ahead of time to prepare for this process:
- ✓ Update your CV: Make sure to include all work, community service and student teaching experiences. Include any other related experiences and/or education that demonstrate your skill set. *A sample template is available on our website: www.GlobalServicesInEducation.com*. Make note that most international schools require a recent picture on your CV.
- ✓ Create a cover letter template: Your cover letter should include why you are interested in teaching internationally, your educational philosophy, your work and leadership experiences and what makes you a viable candidate for an international placement. We suggest creating a template that can be easily modified for different schools in different regions. *A sample template is available on our website: www.GlobalServicesInEducation.com*.

  The majority of your cover letter will stay the same for each school. The only changes will be your introductory paragraph and the closing statements. Your

introductory paragraph should match your profile with the position's needs. The closing statements should reaffirm your commitment and interest in the specific position.

> **GREAT IDEA:** A great "first sentence" for your introductory paragraph is: "I believe my profile and vision matches needs you have for an experienced and internationally-minded teacher." Then go on to highlight specific examples of this.

- ✓ Request official copies of your transcripts, degrees and teaching certificates. It may be easier and more cost effective to request a few copies at once so you will not need to keep repeating this process.

- ✓ Obtain at least a dozen RECENT passport photos including a digital copy. These photos will be used for a range of purposes that may include submitting your visa and residency applications, opening a bank account, obtaining telephone services, etc.

- ✓ Request a letter of reference from your current referees*. You should obtain a letter of reference from up to three past supervisors and other credible people who can demonstrate your professional and personal integrity. The letters should define your relationship, cite strengths applicable to the international context and highlight your adaptability to different situations.

- ✓ Request a "proof of work" letter from your current employer. This letter should include dates of employment, job title and job responsibilities. A "proof of work" letter should be written by your current supervisor on company letterhead with a company stamp if applicable. It should also include an original signature. *A sample template is available on our website: www.GlobalServicesInEducation.com.*

- ✓ Create folders on your computer so you can easily access important files and documents. Create folders for:
    - Scanned copies of past evaluations
    - Reference letters including a list of referees with correct contact information
    - Work samples
    - Cover letters (saved by school name)

- Digital copy of your passport, passport photo and drivers' license
- CV including a personal statement with your educational philosophy
- Copies of transcripts/teaching licenses/teaching certifications

* A person who writes a reference for you will commonly be referred to as a "referee" in the international community.

✓ Do your homework. Study different regions with an open mind and discover where you would be willing to work and live. Your research may include internet searches, school websites, books on travel and contact with established social networks. Also, check your country's travel advisory services.

GREAT IDEA: Get a range of opinions and perspectives from family and friends. Balance that with your needs and lifestyle choices.

✓ Create a checklist. This checklist should include all of the things that are important to you, professionally and personally, in relation to international employment.

Possible things to include on your checklist:

- Salary
- Savings potential
- Accommodations
- Package inclusions
- Religion
- Personal interests and hobbies
- Lifestyle (local laws and customs)
- Location (accessibility, nearby travel destinations, etc.)
- School's philosophy
- Travel allowances
- Professional opportunities

Before signing any contract you should revisit your checklist and make sure that this is the right decision for you.

Common steps in the application process:

Prescreening: Most recruiting companies have a prescreening process that includes an application, extensive reference checks and submission of your educational philosophy. You will be asked to provide professional and personal references. This may include references from students and parents of students you have taught in the past. In addition, you may be asked to submit a written narrative clearly describing and demonstrating your educational philosophy.

This will allow the recruiter to appropriately match you with schools and regions that share your philosophy.

Initial interview:

There are three common interview models:

➢ Traditional Recruiting Model:

This would involve you making direct contact with your school of choice without any additional support or assistance.

- o Pro: It can be relatively inexpensive for you.
- o Con: Most international schools use agents to help filter and manage a very time-consuming and competitive recruitment process.
- o Con: It is helpful for you to have an experienced agent watching out for your best interests in a field you may know little about.

➢ Recruitment Fair Model:

Some international companies have recruiting fairs for you to meet and interview with directors face-to-face.

- o Pro: You are able to network in person with other international teaching candidates.
- o Con: This involves you paying your own travel expenses and hotel accommodations.
- o Con: With large numbers of people all competing for interview opportunities, some candidates may find the recruitment fair overwhelming.

➢ Technology-Driven Model:

Online interviewing processes are both time and cost effective as you do not have to travel to recruitment fairs.

- o Pro: This model moves international interviewing into the 21st century. It allows you to interview "face-to-face" via VoIP (Voice over Internet Protocol) or other online programs.
- o Pro: Because you do not have to travel to an interview, costs are kept to a minimum.

> o Con: If you are not comfortable with creating relationships online, you may find the networking aspect of this model difficult.

Interview:

Items to provide during your interview (email in advance if the interview is online):

- CV with cover letter (cover letter should be school specific)
- Letters of reference (at least three)
- Portfolio (digital or hard copy): work samples, past evaluations, additional photos of you working in a learning environment, etc.

You may be asked questions that are not commonly asked in your home country. Here is a list of commonly asked international interview questions and an explanation as to why they are asked:

- Do you smoke? Some international schools do not hire smokers.
- How old are you? Some countries have visa restrictions based on age.
- Are you married? Are you traveling with a partner? Teaching spouses/partners can save an international school money through accommodations. If you are married or traveling with a non-teaching partner, this is an added cost for international schools since housing for both you and your partner must be provided.
- How many children do you have? International schools usually provide tuition for your school-aged children.
- What is your sexual preference? Homosexuality is considered illegal in some countries.

You are moving to a country with different cultures, beliefs, norms and laws. What you may describe as an awkward question, may not be in the host country. Talk to your recruiting agent to find a school and/or region that fits your profile.

Questions *YOU* should ask during an interview:

- SPECIFIC questions about the school and region. Remember; you should NOT go into an interview unprepared. You should be fully aware of the location of the school, basic facts about the country or region, and knowledge of any school information available on the Internet.

GREAT IDEA: Prepare for your upcoming interview! Our book *A+ Interviewing for Educators* is a comprehensive guide to interview questions and answers. A "must have" even for the experienced teacher!

Optional second or third interview: Some international schools may have you interview a second or even third time with the same interviewer or additional school leaders. If this is the case, provide all of the same documents as you did in your first interview. Be prepared for more specific and detailed questions.

 Offer of contract: In the international community a verbal agreement is binding. Once offered a position ask for a 48-hour window to weigh your options and decide if the school is a good fit for you. Talk to your recruiting agent and read your contract thoroughly. Discuss the job offer not only with your recruiting agent, but with family and friends as well. This is an opportunity to hear a range of different opinions - some informed and some not. This is all healthy and an important part of the process helping you to thoughtfully consider all aspects of your choice. All of these factors will help you make an informed decision. *See our Contract section for specific things to look for in a contract.*

Arrival: Many international schools have you book your own flights and you are reimbursed upon arrival. Most schools reimburse an economy-class flight on the most direct route from your nearest major airport from home of residence. (Remember to keep all receipts!) Check with your school as most schools pay up to a predetermined value.   By booking your own flights, this allows you the flexibility to choose your flight details.

It is essential that you communicate your complete and up-to-date flight information to your school leaders so they can prepare for your arrival.

Questions to ask regarding arrival:
- When will my accommodations be available?
- When will I be reimbursed for my flight?
- Will someone meet me at the airport? How will I recognize them?
- Will I have immediate access to the Internet and telephone upon arrival?
- What documents do I need on hand to present on arrival?
- What other transitional assistance will be available to help me? (Most reputable international schools will have a comprehensive orientation program.)

Attesting Documents: Attestation is the authentication of official documents. If your school asks for attested documents, there may be companies that take care of this for you or your university may provide this service. This may take time and different

countries may have different processes. Documents that may require attestation include copies of your diplomas/degrees (high school and college), teaching certificates, children's birth certificates if applicable, and/or marriage certificate if applicable.

If you have more than one degree, you may need only to attest the degree you are using for the purpose of your employment. For example, if you have a marketing degree and a music degree and you will be teaching music, you may only need to attest your music degree. If you have any questions about your degrees or attestation, ask your school leadership team.

Note: If you cannot locate an original copy of your degree and have to order a new one from your university, remember that replacement degrees take time and you should plan accordingly.

Keep the receipts for all attestations. This includes receipts from companies offering attestation services. Your school may reimburse you up to a certain amount as long as all receipts are presented.

Attitude: Remember you are no longer living and working in your home country. To be successful, you have to be open-minded and flexible. See differences as the exciting opportunities they are! Things may be very different than what you are used to, but this is part of the adventure of living abroad.

Athens, Greece, *Acropolis*

-B-

Baggage: International teachers are encouraged to buy household and personal items in their host country because international schools will rarely provide substantial freight relocation allowances. In some cases they might provide a settling allowance to assist with local purchases. You will often find that it is less expensive to buy new household items once you arrive.

Note: Be careful with baggage restrictions if you have a stopover. You might find that if you check in three suitcases at your city of departure and you stopover and have to check in again, your baggage allowance may change leading to excess baggage charges. Check this with your airlines. *See our Shipping section for more information on shipping freight.*

> **GREAT IDEA: As you pack your bags, make sure you keep a checklist of what is in each piece of luggage. This way if your luggage is lost, you can easily fill out the claim form listing items and approximate values.**

Balance: Take time out for you. You are living in a foreign country…experience it and embrace it! Get to know the locals. Safely try things you have never tried before. Work with purpose and diligence and live the same way. Make sure you take time out for yourself to do the things you enjoy doing outside of work.

Banking: Your school will most likely help you set up a local bank account in your host country. Be sure you understand the account features and benefits. This local account will allow you to withdraw funds in local currency as most schools will deposit your salary directly into this account on a monthly basis. You will be responsible for this account so learn how to complete wire transfers, credit card payments if applicable and understand any fees and charges associated with the account.

If you have financial commitments at home, investigate and establish a simple process for wire transfers and online banking if available. Note that wire transfer fees may be charged to the sender's and receiver's accounts. Consider this when calculating the amount of money you need to transfer.

Black Balling: The international education world is surprisingly small. It is not uncommon for directors and headmasters to communicate regularly within their networks to find good teachers and to warn about teachers with unethical practices.

It is important to note that by verbally accepting an offer at an international school, your word is your bond. As in any work place or industry, it is ethical that if you accept an offer, you honor that commitment. If you do change your mind about a previously accepted position, it is up to you to negotiate out of the agreement in a similarly ethical and professional manner. You should be aware that you may damage your reputation both formally and informally by your demonstrated behaviors. International schools acknowledge that there is an expectation of ethical hiring practices for them also.

Blogs: Social networking sites are valuable resources for connecting people and learning about countries and schools. Keep in mind that many highly regarded websites are not filtered and can represent loud minorities as well as broad perspectives. Weigh your different sources of information so that you are getting a balanced picture and are fully informed. Contributing to these sites in a positive and professional manner can help other international teachers and travelers. However, posting biased or culturally insensitive statements can mislead and offend.

GREAT IDEA: While blogging, take the opportunity to contribute positive comments and recommendations when they are deserving.

Boarding Schools: Some international schools have boarding facilities so you may have the option of living on campus in exchange for additional duties. Food and accommodations may be provided at no extra expense to you while living in the boarding facilities. With that, some boarding schools may offer you less space and possibly no kitchen area. *See our Accommodations section for questions to ask regarding boarding school accommodations.*

Books: Books may not always be easily accessible or may be more expensive than in your home country. We suggest that you bring along your favorite books or consider e-books as an alternative. Teachers in some schools set up book exchanges or you might find that this already exists in your expatriate community in local coffee shops.

Budget: It is imperative you create a budget that guides and monitors your spending. Because some international schools do not have retirement plans, you need to take personal control of your financial future. Be in control of your spending. You are embarking on an adventure that could allow you to save a lot of money in a short amount of time.

Beijing, China, *Summer Palace*

-C-

Car: In some regions you will find that taxis, city buses and other forms of transportation are more convenient than having the hassle of your own vehicle. Check with other teachers and expats in your area and make an informed decision before purchasing a vehicle. In some countries leasing may be a more viable, cheaper option as well. If you choose to drive, investigate registration, insurance and drivers' license requirements. Do not assume that all countries' systems and regulations are the same.

Care Packages: Family and friends may send you "care packages" from time to time with your favorite things from home. Make sure that people know what they can and cannot send, but encourage this thoughtful gesture. Some items that might have customs' restrictions are liquids, perfumes, food products, items made of wood, etc.

Cash: Upon arrival you should have some money readily available in case you need to access it fast. It is also suggested that you have immediate access to cash, credit or travelers' checks in case an emergency situation arises. Do not keep all of your cash, credit or travelers' checks in the same place. It may also be a good idea to purchase a small safe for installation in your apartment.

Cell Phones: If you are bringing a cell phone from home, you may need to get it "unlocked" before using it in your host country. Check with your local provider and tell them you are relocating overseas. They should be able to assist you with this service.

Cell phone plans are structured differently in each country. Talk to other expats at your school to decide the best plan for your needs.

GREAT IDEA: Make sure to turn off roaming when traveling outside of your coverage area to avoid excess data charges.

Certification: It is important to keep all teacher certifications up to date. Check with your department of education to ensure you are meeting certification requirements while you are overseas. Keep in mind that even if certification is not needed at your current international school, it may be required at your next. It is much easier to keep certificates current than to start the process from the beginning. Also, make sure to keep extra copies of your certification and also keep a copy available digitally.

Children's Records: If you are traveling with children, make sure you bring their birth certificates, school records, copies of health records and a list of past medications and immunizations. Since ages and corresponding grade levels may be different in different countries, it is also suggested that you have your child's teacher(s) write a letter describing your child's academic profile. This will assist in proper grade placement.

Classifieds: Within most expat communities people are regularly moving in and out of the country. Use this to your advantage. Check memo boards, internet classified ads and bulletin boards at your school for great "garage sale" deals. Buying second-hand items is not only practical and cost effective, but it is also commonplace in the international community.

Clauses: Your contract is a negotiated agreement between you and your employer. Your contract includes clauses that represent what is expected of both parties. You need to read your contract carefully and make sure you agree with each individual clause. Also check for clauses that could negate other portions of your contract. It is a good idea to have a third party read your contract as well. *See our Contract section for questions to ask.*

Clothes: It is important to respect local customs and expectations in your host country. Before packing a lot of clothes you aren't going to wear, find out what local customs are. For example, in some countries women cannot wear shorts or sleeveless clothes.

Clothing Sizes: Sizes are labeled differently in different parts of the world. To determine your appropriate sizes, see table below:

International Clothing Sizes – Women

Women's Dresses and Suits								
United States	6	8	10	12	14	16	18	20
UK	8	10	12	14	16	18	20	22
Europe (Italy)	38	40	42	44	46	48	50	52
Europe	34	36	38	40	42	44	46	48
Europe (Spain and	36	38	40	42	44	46	48	50
Women's Shoes								
United States	5 ½	6	6 ½	7	7 ½	8	8 ½	9
UK	3	3 ½	4	4 ½	5	5 ½	6	6 ½
Europe	35 ½	36	37	37 ½	38	38 ½	40 ½	40
Japan	21 ½	22 ½	23	23 ½	24	24 ½	25	25 ½

International Clothing Sizes – Men

Men's Suits and Coasts								
United States	36	38	40	42	44	46	48	50
UK	36	38	40	42	44	46	48	50
Europe	46	48	50/52	54	56	58/60	62	64
Men's Shirts								
United States	14	14 ½	15	15 ½	16	16 ½	17	17 ½
UK	14	14 ½	15	15 ½	16	16 ½	17	17 ½
Europe	35	36/37	38	39/40	41	42/43	44	45
Men's Shoes								
United States	7	8	9	10	11	12	13	14
UK	6	7	8	9	10	11	12	13
Europe	39	40 ½	42/43	43/44	44½/	46	47	48
Japan	25	26	27	28	29	30	31	32

Note: Sizes can vary considerably between regions and designs

Communication: Effective communication is imperative in all school communities; however, there may be additional communication barriers in schools where English is the second language. Identify strategies early to ensure that parents have access to their child's progress and achievement. Some ways to achieve this include using translators and creating comment banks of key phrases in the host language.

Also be aware of non-verbal communications such as gestures and body language. For example, in some Asian countries nodding your head may mean "no" instead of "yes."

GREAT IDEA: Many online and smartphone applications are surprisingly effective in helping you with simple translations.

Computer: Most schools will provide you with access to a computer during your working hours. However, you are encouraged to travel with your own laptop/netbook as this is important for your independence and with communicating with family and friends back home. Because some programs may be difficult to download in certain countries, make sure all relevant programs are installed before leaving home, including a virus protection program(s).

Consulates: Immediately upon arrival, register with your home country's consulate. You may be able to do this online. Most consulates will provide regular email updates with travel advice, weather forecasts and provide additional levels of support for you.

Contracts: The interviewing process can be a stressful one and the final stage of accepting a contract is crucial. Most teaching contracts are signed for two years and administrator contracts are signed for three years. It is important to note that some international schools will first make you a verbal offer. An accepted verbal offer is considered binding as the school will then cease interviewing other candidates. If you are offered a position and you are unsure if you want to accept the position, be honest and say you need more time to decide. Schools know that this is a big decision and that candidates are interviewing for many jobs. Take time to talk to your family and make the best decision for you.

Before you sign any contract, it is imperative that you read it carefully. You may choose to also have a third party look over your contract and speak directly with your recruiting agent.

GREAT IDEA: Ask your recruiting agent to help you make contact with a lawyer in your host country. This will ensure that your contract meets local labor laws as well as your own expectations.

Have a checklist of things that are important to you and make certain that your contract addresses these key issues. *See our Application Process section for a sample checklist.*

Questions to ask about your contract:
- Salary:
    - How often am I paid?
    - How much am I paid?
    - In what currency am I paid?
    - Will my salary be directly deposited into my local bank account?
    - Will I be required to pay taxes in my host country? If so, how?

- Insurance:
    - What does my medical insurance include? (vision? dental?)
    - Is my medical insurance valid worldwide?
    - Does the school pay 100% of my medical insurance?
    - Is disability insurance available?

- Is life insurance available?

- Flights Home:
    - How many flights does the school pay for? (start and end of contract? annual flights?)
    - Is the entire cost of my flight home paid for?
    - Will the school consider providing cash in lieu of a flight?

- Housing:
    - Is housing provided or is there a housing allowance given?
    - If housing is provided, will I be required to have a roommate?
    - Where is housing located?
    - What facilities are available on or near property?
    - Are my utilities paid for by the school? If yes, which ones?

- Transport:
    - Is transport provided to and from work?

- Probationary Period:
    - What is the length of the probationary period?
    - What are the terms of the probationary period?

- Obligations:
    - What is the length of my contract? Am I able to renew?
    - What are the terms of agreement within the contract for both parties?
    - Does my contract meet local labor laws?
    - When does the school year begin and end?
    - When am I required to be in the host country?
    - What is the school calendar?

- Family (if applicable):
    - Will you assist my non-teaching partner in finding a job?
    - Do you pay for my family's relocation flights and medical insurance?
    - Will my child's school tuition be paid by the school?
    - Is housing provided for my family?
    - What if I get pregnant? Will my newborn child be covered?

- Job Description:
    - What are the expectations for me sponsoring extracurricular activities?
    - What are the standard work hours?
    - What are my responsibilities outside of the classroom?

> **GREAT IDEA: If you are asked to sign an additional contract in the host country's language, have the documented translated into your language before signing.**

Conversion Rates: Be aware that conversion rates vary. Just because an agent offers "no fees" does not mean you are getting a great deal. Agents receive commission either directly through fees or indirectly through an inflated conversion rate.

Converters: A converter for electrical appliances simply converts the plug to fit into a different pronged socket. International multi-country converters are easily purchased in most travel and electronic shops. Be aware that a converter alone will not adjust voltage of an electronic device. *See our section on Transformers for adjusting voltage.*

Converting Money: You may want to convert some money before you board the airplane to leave home. It is suggested that you have enough cash to get through the first 24-48 hours after you arrive in your host country. Most airports offer this service although they often have a poorer rate of exchange. Your local bank may be able to assist you with this service.

> **GREAT IDEA: If you cannot get your host country's local currency in advance, take US dollars or another major currency.**

Cost of Living: There are many websites that provide cost of living indexes for most major cities around the world. Depending on your personal lifestyle choices, these indexes can be misleading. These indexes are calculated on general profiles rather than the profile and lifestyle choices of international teachers. Connecting through social networks with people who are currently living in the country you are investigating remains to be one of your most reliable sources of information.

> **GREAT IDEA: To calculate your own "cost of living index," ask your school contact the local prices of your five most commonly purchased items.**

Credit Cards: You should contact your bank and place a "travel alert" on your credit card(s) so that the bank does not suspend your access while overseas. If you want a credit card, apply before leaving home. It may be more difficult to obtain a credit card in some host countries. Also be aware that some credit card companies may charge an additional fee for overseas spending.

Criminal Records: Most schools, recruitment companies and visa processes will require a complete and formal check of any criminal records. If you have a criminal record, disclose this to your recruiting agent immediately. Depending on the offense, this may not be a "deal-breaker" if handled in an open and honest manner.

Culture Shock: To help avoid culture shock, talk to people already living in your host country. Start to build connections through international social networks or through school leadership/contacts well in advance. Also, pack a few items that easily fit in your luggage that will remind you of home, e.g., a digital frame with photos already loaded (don't forget your adapter/transformer), pictures, music, favorite snack (if food can be brought into the country), etc.

Reading books, like this one, will help you better prepare yourself for your international move.

GREAT IDEA: Ease yourself into your new environment by experiencing your host country a little at a time. You don't have to discover everything in a day!

Current Events: It is important to keep up to date on current events in your host country, home country and countries you plan to travel. There are many online news and travel websites to assist you with this. Some news websites also give you the option to subscribe to regular email updates. In addition to this, always check the Internet for the latest travel warnings and travel advice.

Curriculum: Most international schools follow American, International Baccalaureate (IB) or British curriculum models. Investigate each school's curriculum model and more specifically ask the school what their curriculum model looks like within the school's context. If you don't know the curriculum model well, demonstrate confidence and the capacity to adapt quickly.

Customs and Border Control: Research what you are and are not permitted to bring into your host country. Having an illegal item in your luggage could bring penalties and delay you getting your things. Your school may provide some of these details in an orientation handbook.

Chengdu, China, *Giant Panda Breeding Research Base*

-D-

Differentiation: Just as differentiation is important in your home school, it is equally important in an international environment. Given the characteristics of most international schools, differentiation of curriculum and student learning should be a high priority for you. Your school leaders will expect you to implement best practices to reach and engage all learners in each of your lessons.

> **GREAT IDEA: Convert all of your teaching resources into electronic format. Bring them with you on a portable hard drive.**

Disabilities: International schools may not be designed or equipped to support staff or students with certain disabilities. If you have a disability, be open with your recruiting agent to be sure that the school in which you are applying can meet your needs.

Discipline Issues: Just because your environment has changed, it doesn't mean that key and basic fundamentals for good student management are any different. Discipline issues can be avoided by engaging students in well-planned lessons. If discipline issues persist, follow best practices regarding classroom management. Make sure to keep parents and administration informed of any problems you may be encountering.

Discrimination: Remember you are no longer bound by the laws and beliefs of your home country. What you may consider discrimination, may be considered lawful in your host country and acceptable for international school hiring practices. For example, some international schools may prefer to hire married, non-smoking couples. This may seem like a discriminatory practice to some, but it is perfectly acceptable in the international community.

Doctors: Be assured that most major international cities have high-quality international medical centers and services comparable in standards to your home country. You should ask expatriates in your area for doctor referrals.

> **GREAT IDEA: Before leaving home, check with your primary physician for advice on specialist health care in your host country.**

Documents: You will be required to supply a number of documents both to the school and other organizations depending on the region you will be living. When the documents are requested, send them immediately. Not only does this demonstrate

your professionalism, but it is important for you to realize that some processes may take longer than you would predict or longer than they would in your home country. You may be required to supply originals, copies or certified or authenticated copies. We also recommend that you have all copies in digital form as well. *See our Application Process section for more information.*

The following list covers a range of documents that you may be required to produce. Plan ahead so you have them easily accessible as required.

- ➤ Birth certificate (all family members if applicable)
- ➤ Passport
- ➤ Marriage certificate (if applicable)
- ➤ Degrees and transcripts
- ➤ Teaching certifications
- ➤ "Proof of work" letter
- ➤ Immunizations (if applicable)
- ➤ Medical records (specific format required for different regions)
- ➤ Criminal history check
- ➤ CV
- ➤ Letters of reference
- ➤ Visa (your school will provide advice)

Dress: All regions will have different cultural expectations for dress. You should be conservative in dress and respectful of your host country's expectations. Schools will provide advice regarding dress in your work setting. *See also our Clothes and Local Dress sections.*

Driver's License: Some host countries may require an International Driver's Permit (IDP) which may be available in your home country at low cost; others may require you to get a new license under the host country's laws and regulations. Research this well in advance as this may require a waiting period.

Drugs: Rules about bringing drugs/medicines into a country and levels of accessibility are different in different regions. In terms of accessibility, some drugs/medicines may be more accessible and others much more restricted. Be sure to take extra precautions and know what is legal and illegal in your host country. In regard to illegal drugs, be aware that the consequences for illegal drug use in many countries can be quite severe.

DVDs: Different regions use different broadcast formats for video. The United States favors a format called NTSC (National Television Standards Committee), while Europe, Australia and parts of Asia use a competing format called PAL (Phase Alternating Line). You should be aware that DVDs might not play on a competing format. If you purchase a DVD player in your host country, consider the format of your DVDs or purchase an international or universal player that will play both formats.

Dubai, UAE, *Palm Leaf Development*

-E-

Electronic Equipment: Be aware that different countries have different voltage. Don't make the expensive mistake of plugging a 120-volt appliance into a 220-volt power socket without using a transformer. It could be both a costly and dangerous mistake. *See our sections on Adaptors, Transformers and Voltage.*

Emergency Numbers: Upon arrival in your host country, it is important that you identify and store emergency numbers (English). Your consulate, school and new friends can assist you in locating these numbers in the event that you need emergency assistance.

> **GREAT IDEA: Save emergency numbers in your cell phone for all of your travel destinations as most emergency situations cannot be predicted. Tag the numbers with the name of the relevant city or country.**

End of Contract: You will have committed to a contract that is most likely two years. The school will assume that you will complete your contract in full. Should you have a significant reason or emergency that requires you to end your contract early, be aware of possible penalties as well as obligations and expectations of your employer. Check your contract for specific details.

Possible questions to ask regarding end of contract:
- When do I have to give notice if I am not renewing my contract?
- Is there an option for me to renew my contract early? (Some schools may offer a bonus.)
- If I decide not to renew my contract, what leave do I have available for the recruiting process?
- In relation to my accommodations, what are the expectations prior to departure?
- What are the exit procedures in regards to school matters?
- What are the procedures for canceling my visa, closing bank accounts, etc.?

> **GREAT IDEA: Prior to your departure, sell household items that you have purchased to current teachers or expats in your community.**

English as a Second Language: English will be the primary language of instruction in most international schools. However, English may be the second language of some of

your students. You should understand the needs of these students and plan your lessons accordingly. If this is new to you, network with colleagues in advance and begin to identify best practices and ideas.

Evaluation Process: Most schools will have a probation and performance evaluation process. It is important for you to fully understand how you will be assessed and what the school's expectations are for your performance. Follow your contract, but also all school policies as well. *See Performance Review for more information.*

Questions to ask regarding the school's evaluation process:
- How long is my probationary period?
- Who will be my supervisor?
- What is the school's criteria and evaluation process?
- Is there a mentoring or support program?

Exercise: It is important to live a healthy lifestyle. When work demands are high, that is when we need our body to be healthy - both physically and emotionally. Keep exercise in your daily routine as an important strategy to stay healthy and balanced.

GREAT IDEA: Living in a different country may not be an obstacle but actually an opportunity to establish new healthy behaviors. Try tai chi in Asia, yoga in India or rugby in Europe.

Expatriate Services: There are professional services available to assist you in relocating but some might be costly. Use your school contacts and social networks to assist your move and answer any questions you may have.

Expenses: You are living away from your home country, using a different currency and making different spending choices. Create a budget and track expenses early so that you can quickly adapt and monitor your savings plan. Consider both your daily expenditure and major items you are saving to purchase. For example, your living expenses may be low, but traveling internationally may be more costly. Plan ahead to maximize your savings. *See also our Budget, Finances and Managing Expenses sections.*

Expectations: Like in any school, your school leadership team will establish and communicate teacher expectations. International students and parents expect high academic standards, rigorous curriculum and highly-effective communication. Teachers will be expected to communicate proactively and often to parents. Most parents are fully committed to the parent-teacher relationship and appreciate regular feedback

regarding their child's performance. Also, check with your school leaders to ask about additional duties you may be required to lead. You may be expected to coach and/or sponsor extracurricular activities.

Experience: There is a job for everyone. It is a matter of matching your profile and experience with the needs of the school. A highly-effective recruiting agent will help you identify these schools and pursue your ideal job. Know your strengths and weaknesses, research different schools and regions and commit to the process.

Expertise: During the application process be sure to clearly communicate your greatest strengths and how they match the profile of the school. International schools want the best teachers that fit their needs. With that, it is not unusual in some environments (especially smaller schools) that teachers are asked to teach a range of different subjects for all grade levels. Have a clear understanding of your teaching assignment, either specific or general, before you sign your contract.

Egypt, Pyramids

-F-

Families: International school environments provide wonderful opportunities for your family to travel and experience new cultures. Your children will benefit through this exposure to new people, lifestyles and ideas and make great strides towards becoming globally-minded citizens.

To help your children adapt to their new environment, you may want to consider the following suggestions:

- Bring familiar items, including favorite toys and books.
- Connect quickly with other families with children.
- Speak openly with your children about the transition to your new home.
- Encourage regular communication with family and friends at home.
- Quickly establish a structured routine in your host country.

Questions to ask regarding moving your family abroad:

- Will my child(ren)'s school tuition be included in my package?
- Will flights for my family be covered?
- Will insurance be provided for my family?
- How will my child's grade level be determined?
- Are there many other teachers at the school with families?
- Are children's books, clothing and toys easily accessible?
- Are there daycare and babysitting services available?

GREAT IDEA: Bring a surprise "care package" that your child(ren) can open on arrival from family and friends back home.

Female Items: Some countries may not sell a wide range of feminine hygiene products. Pack a "good supply" of your favorite products or be willing to use what is available. Check with your local contact regarding feminine hygiene options.

Finances: You are moving to a different region with a different cost of living and potential lifestyle choices. Plan for your retirement by monitoring your finances. *Refer to our Banking, Budget and Managing Expenses sections for specific advice.*

First-Aid Kit: It is best to prepare a "traveler's first-aid kit" and a "general purpose first-aid kit" before you leave home. This will ensure that if something happens, you are

already prepared. Most medicines are likely to be available in your host country, but it is important to have them quickly in case of emergency. Your physician should be able to make suggestions of items to include. If you are traveling with prescription medication, make sure you travel with it in the original container and with the original prescription. You should also verify that the medicine and quantity are legal in your host country.

Possible items to include in your first-aid kits:
- ✓ Nausea medicine
- ✓ Anti-inflammatory medicine
- ✓ Bandages (adhesive and non-adhesive)
- ✓ Soap or alcohol preps
- ✓ Hand sanitizer
- ✓ Antibiotic cream
- ✓ Thermometer
- ✓ Non-aspirin pain reliever
- ✓ Cold medicine
- ✓ Diarrhea/Laxative medicine
- ✓ Allergy medicine
- ✓ Antacid
- ✓ Sunscreen
- ✓ Any personal medications you may need

GREAT IDEA: Create a separate kit that is always maintained for traveling rather than day-to-day usage.

Flight Delays: Although it is impossible to prevent flight delays, there are some things you can do to lower your risk of being affected. Choose an early morning flight and choose reasonable lay-over periods so that you are not rushing from one flight to the next. There are sites that allow you to check the history of flights and give you the statistics for on-time travel.

Flights Home: Reputable international schools will reimburse for your relocation flight and a return flight home annually. Many schools will give you the cash value of your annual flight allowance to use at your own discretion. Find out when your allowance is available because you may save money by booking in advance.

Food and Delicacies: Part of the excitement of living in a new and different culture is tasting and experiencing different foods. When offered something unique and it looks freshly-prepared and handled, why not give it a try?

Forbidden Curriculum: Your host country will have unique values, beliefs, histories and traditions. While you will never be expected to adopt the local beliefs and values as your own, you need to respect them. Be careful of making politically-charged statements and statements of judgment. If you feel you may be at risk of exploring sensitive topics in your classroom, always check with your school leadership team about if and how the topic should be approached. An experienced recruiting agent will alert you to any special situations you may encounter in your host country.

Foreign Perceptions: Just as you may have misconceptions about new cultures, be aware that others may have misconceptions about yours also. Be sensitive and understand the possible differences between your host country's values and your own. Learn to celebrate the differences instead of becoming frustrated by them.   Carry yourself with integrity and respect your host country's values and beliefs.

Frankfurt, Germany, *St. Bartholomeus Cathedral*

-G-

Gambling: The various laws of gambling in different countries/regions/states can be found through internet research. These laws may also apply differently regarding online gambling. BE AWARE: Penalties for illegal gambling may be more severe than in your home country.

Geography: Keep an open mind when considering choices of where to work and live. Investigate regions for yourself and avoid overgeneralized or media-created perceptions that may not give you the full picture of the region. Another thing to consider is savings potential. For example, Europe may sound like a great place to live, but your savings potential may be lower.

Things to consider:
- ✓ Climate
- ✓ Savings potential
- ✓ Travel opportunities
- ✓ Gender treatment
- ✓ Lifestyle
- ✓ Safety
- ✓ Adaptability to culture limitations and restraints

> **GREAT IDEA: Consider working in locations with higher savings potential and traveling to more luxurious locations during extended breaks.**

Germs: Your host country may have different hygiene standards and possibly different germs that your body has not come into contact with before. Maintain good hygiene at all times and show precaution that all food you consume is well prepared. Also, use hand sanitizer regularly when soap and water is unavailable.

Gifts: Most schools will have a policy regarding giving and receiving gifts from students and parents. Be aware that there are also cultural differences in regard to gift exchanges. Also, inform family and friends about items that may be restricted or prohibited in your host country.

Gratuity: Different countries have different practices related to tipping and service fees in the areas of taxis, hospitality and other service industries. While in some places it is

expected, in other regions it is considered rude and derogatory. Check with locals in your area to research local practices.

Guests: As a general rule, most international schools will not provide separate accommodations for guests or visitors. Check with your school if guests can stay in your school-provided accommodations. If not, seek alternative options nearby. *See our section on Visitors.*

Galway, Ireland, *Kyleway Abbey*

-H-

Hard Drives: Back-up your files and create two copies; one to travel with you and one to leave at home for added security. This will ensure that even if one hard drive gets lost in the move, you still have a back-up. You can also consider web-based storage systems as an alternative.

Hardship Post: A hardship post is considered an appointment to a less desirable location with lifestyle restrictions. These locations may be attractive to some candidates as they may bring increased salary, higher savings potential and unique lifestyle experiences. While many teachers relish such opportunities, some may find that the reality of the situation is much more difficult than they had presumed.

When considering such posts, take additional time and steps to make sure you are fully informed and aware of safety concerns and restrictions. A well-respected recruiting firm will be able to help you make an informed decision.

Health: When changing countries, climates or cultures, it is important to stay healthy by following commonsense precautions. Arriving healthy and staying healthy should be your goal. Maintain good hygiene, eat healthy foods and get lots of rest.

Health Insurance: Most international schools offer full worldwide medical coverage. Some contracts exclude coverage in certain parts of the world. Do not verbally agree to any employment contract until you see, in writing, what your medical coverage will be. Check to see what is included in your coverage and if there are any additional fees and/or charges. *See our Contracts and Insurance sections for more information.*

Questions to ask regarding medical coverage:
- ✓ Are dental and vision benefits included?
- ✓ In what regions and countries am I covered? Not covered?
- ✓ If I am traveling, does insurance cover any emergency medical treatments needed and/or transport back to my host country?
- ✓ Am I covered if I get injured participating in a high-risk recreational activity, e.g., skydiving, waterskiing, etc.
- ✓ Is there a deductible?
- ✓ What are the limits of the policies?
- ✓ Do I get to choose my own doctors?
- ✓ Do my benefits cover my family?

✓ Can I choose to extend the coverage at my own cost if required?

Hiring Policies: See our section on the Application Process.

Holidays: Each school will create a calendar that reflects the needs of the curriculum and the holidays of the host country. In some cases the school will recognize holidays from different countries depending on affiliations with that country and/or the curriculum it represents. In most cases the school calendar will represent the holidays of the host country. Note that these holidays may or may not reflect your own religious traditions or customs.

Homesickness: It is natural to feel homesick at times, either for people that you miss or for some of the comforts that remind you of home.   Here are some things that may provide support for you:

When you are missing friends and family, try these things:
- Email your friends and family
- Call or use VoIP (Voice over Internet Protocol) to contact your friends and family so you can hear their voices
- Write letters (a somewhat forgotten, thoughtful gesture)
- Write in your journal
- Be active…exercise, go for a walk, explore a new area
- Spend time with your new friends
- Share stories of home

When you are missing the comforts of home, try these things:
- Celebrate your own holidays and traditions no matter where you are
- Get together with fellow expats
- Enjoy a treat from your home country, e.g., ice cream, hamburger, etc.
- Play your favorite music
- Watch a favorite movie
- Create a "game night" with your new friends

Hospitals: Most major international cities will have a hospital of international standards comparable to your home country. Ask your school what local hospitals are preferred by foreign teachers and approved by your insurance company.

Housing: Accommodations can range from apartment living (single or shared) to living on campus.   Check your contract for specific housing descriptions. Some schools may also be able to send photos of locations and interiors. Ask your school what items come as "standard inventory" so you can plan accordingly. *See our Accommodations section for more information.*

Humanitarian: Visiting and living in other countries provides a great opportunity to make a difference globally. Often this may be reflected in the philosophy of your international school. Get involved! This is a great way to "pay it forward." Working internationally is not just a way to travel the world; it is a great way to make a difference. You will be a role model to your students and the school community as an internationally-minded citizen.

Hygiene: Like your mother always told you, wash your hands! It is also helpful to have a bottle of hand sanitizer with you. As simple as that sounds, it is important to remember that not all countries have western standards and guidelines when it comes to cleanliness and food preparations. Only eat food that is freshly prepared and stored. Find out if the tap water is drinkable and if you are unsure, only drink water that is boiled or bottled.

Hong Kong, *The Pavilion of Absolute Perfection*

Immunization and Immunization Records: Part of the visa process in most countries requires having a blood test, chest x-ray and certain immunizations to be completed shortly after arrival. Some of these immunizations are quick and simple but others can take several weeks. If you have had the required immunizations in the past, bring your immunization records with you.

GREAT IDEA: Keep hard copies and electronic copies of all your health records.

Induction: Reputable international schools will provide a thorough induction program to not only the school, but the community as well. What is not covered by the school can be easily covered through your extensive research and solid preparation. Use this as a great opportunity to fully prepare yourself for your life in this new environment. Ask lots of questions and take lots of notes.

Insurance: Most international school's insurance policies will cover worldwide medical care coverage and crisis evacuation costs. Beyond medical insurance, make sure you investigate personal travel and life insurance.

You may also want to investigate insuring your personal belongings. As most international schools pay for your housing, additional insurance on material things would be your responsibility. This policy may need to be purchased in your host country.

Another important insurance to consider is travel insurance. This will rarely be covered within your school's insurance policy. You can purchase travel insurance "as you go" or on an annual basis. Depending on your frequency of travel, annual travel insurance may prove to be more cost effective. This can be purchased online or via most travel agencies.

Intellectual Property: Teachers need to be reminded that any ideas or creations while employed by the school, either tangible or intangible, are considered to be the intellectual property of the school. It is your professional responsibility to collaborate, share and leave materials that have been created.

International Day: International schools often celebrate their international-mindedness by asking students and staff to dress in a "national costume" and share customs and traditions from their home countries. This is a chance to embrace other cultures while being patriotic to your home country. When choosing your "national costume," think about different ways you can represent your country and/or region. Prepare for this before leaving your home country.

GREAT IDEA: Bring large numbers of inexpensive souvenirs to share with your students. It is also fun to share songs, games, photos and stories from your home country.

International-Mindedness: Schools will want to see this both in your written philosophy and your personal behaviors. You need to think deeply and sincerely about what this means to you. International-mindedness is not "tolerating" differences. A true sense of international-mindedness is embracing and celebrating our unique beliefs, customs and traditions. For many international schools they see this as what sets them apart from traditional schools.

Internet: Different countries have different levels of restrictions in regards to the Internet. Some websites and services may be blocked. For example, Facebook, Twitter and YouTube are blocked in some countries. The use of a VPN (Virtual Private Network) account can avoid this problem, but be aware that this may not be legal in your host country or your home country. *See also our VPN section.*

Many teachers use their school's internet connection to access their private e-mail account. Check your school's policy on use of internet and personal email.

Internships: Many international schools will offer internship programs to high-quality graduates. This is a great opportunity to experience international living while working with talented teachers in a culturally-rich environment. In many cases, internships can lead to future employment and broaden your skills and experiences. Compensation will vary from school to school.

Interview: It is important to be well prepared for your interview. Have a clear understanding of where the school is located, basic facts about the region, your own educational philosophy and the school's vision and key priorities. A good recruiting company can help you prepare for this process. *See our Application Process section for interviewing tips.*

Isles of Scilly, United Kingdom

-J-

Jet lag: It is important to adjust to your new time zone as quickly as possible. Adjustment best occurs by taking short naps, eating light foods and drinking lots of water. During the daytime expose yourself to natural sunlight (using sunscreen, of course) and stay active. At nighttime draw the shades and avoid use of electronic equipment, such as computers, that may stimulate you. Be aware that jet lag may affect your mood, appetite and reduce your immunity towards illness.

Job Application/Interview: See our Application Process and Interview sections.

Job Opportunities: Most international schools have next school year's jobs advertised by December; however, many will begin posting as early as October. For the most part, schools post job opportunities on their website and with recruiting companies. Since it is virtually impossible to check every school's website and also check their credibility as a "good school," we strongly recommend working through a reputable recruiting agent. This will allow you to stay current on all jobs available that match your profile, make informed decisions and answer any questions you may have during the process.

Journals: It is a good idea to document your experiences and travel by keeping a journal. A journal provides an outlet for reflection and a vehicle to "frame" your experiences.

> **GREAT IDEA: Using your journal entries, create a regular newsletter for family and friends back home.**

Justice: In your host country, you will not necessarily be protected by the laws of your home country. Upon arrival in your host country, contact your local consulate and/or embassy and register to ensure you have easy access to the services they provide. If you are in need of legal support, travel advice or emergency assistance while overseas, your consulate or embassy can assist you in finding help.

Java, Indonesia, *Borobudur*

-K-

Keys: You may decide to keep a storage unit in your home country or have other items under lock and key. If so, make sure your family or a reliable friend has an extra key. You are a long way from home and you never know when you may need access to your things.

Kitchen: As standard kitchen equipment varies in different regions, do not assume you will have an oven or other appliances to which you have grown accustomed. If you are choosing to live in a boarding facility, you may not have access to a kitchen or kitchenette. *See our Accommodations and Boarding Schools sections for more information.*

Kunming, China, Shilin Stone Forest

-L-

Languages: Regardless of where you are choosing to relocate, English is the primary language of most international schools. It is not essential to know how to speak the native language of your host country, but this is a great opportunity to learn a different language. You will find it easier to communicate and embrace the local culture by learning simply greetings and key phrases. You may choose to take local classes or even employ a language tutor. You can also ask local staff to help you with translations. Phrase books and smartphone and computer applications are also wonderful tools.

> **GREAT IDEA: Try to learn (and use) one new word each day.**

Learning curve: Teaching and living internationally is great professional development within itself. You are able to share best practices with teachers from all over the world. As you learn new ways of teaching, be open to modifying your own teaching styles and methods. Take this opportunity to embrace your new professional learning community. It represents the best teachers and teaching practices from all over the world.

Legal: Your local consulate or embassy will play a role in helping you maintain your international rights as they apply in your host country. However, it is imperative that you understand your host country's laws and expectations as you are not protected by your home country's laws. With that, make certain you understand your host country's laws before you sign your contract. If you need legal assistance, contact your consulate or embassy immediately. They cannot provide the assistance directly but can put you in touch with recommended legal firms.

Lifestyle: The concept of work-hard, play-hard is synonymous with international teaching environments. Professional educators have high expectations and work hard throughout the school year. When it comes to holidays, you will enjoy wonderful travel opportunities and a well-earned break!

Links: For helpful information and access to resources, visit us at *www.GlobalServicesInEducation.com*.

Liquor: Different regions have different philosophies about consumption of alcohol. In some regions, consuming alcohol in public is illegal. You should have complete knowledge and respect for all laws in your host country.

Living Conditions: Some international schools will be able to provide you with photos or videos of "standard" housing for teachers and staff. A high standard of living will not always look the same in every country. For example, in some countries one-bedroom apartments are the norm while in other countries one-bedroom apartments are extremely rare. Before signing your contract, make sure you are in agreement with your living conditions. *See our Accommodations and Housing sections for more information and questions to ask regarding living conditions.*

Local Dress: Dress choices are best made after researching your host country and understanding the norms of everyday living. For example, in some countries women who bare their arms or legs are looked down upon. Even if your beliefs are different, you should understand and respect those of your host country. Respectably live within these boundaries.

Local Laws: Understand the local laws of your host country. In some countries there will be specific laws about the nature of relationships, gender, practice of religion and other lifestyle freedoms you may have in your home country. Know and understand the local laws of your host country before you sign your contract.

Loneliness: Your relocation to a new country may begin with hectic planning and excitement. However, the transition can be stressful as you may not fully anticipate the effects this change may have on such things as anxiety, moods and even loneliness. Foreigners abroad can counter these feelings by actively pursuing relationships within immediate networks and beyond. Reach out to others and get involved.

GREAT IDEA: Find the local places that expatriates meet on a social basis. If one does not exist already, create one!

Luggage: Be careful with baggage restrictions if you have a stopover. You might find that if you check in three suitcases at your city of departure and you stopover and have to check in again, your baggage allowance may change leading to excess baggage charges. Check this with your airlines. *See our Baggage section for more information.*

GREAT IDEA: Attach a brightly colored ribbon to each piece of your luggage. This will help you easily identify your luggage at baggage claim.

London, England, *Big Ben*

-M-

Maid Services: In some countries maid services may be cheaper and more easily available than in your home country. Finding these services by referral or through a reputable company remains your best bet.

> **GREAT IDEA: Purchase a small safe to store your valuables, including passport, work visa, jewelry, medical records and other valuables.**

Mail Services: See our Postal Services section.

Malaria: Although you cannot be vaccinated against malaria, you can protect yourself by applying mosquito repellent or staying indoors during late evenings when mosquitoes tend to be out. Anti-malaria medication is also available. If you feel you are at risk, contact a doctor immediately.

Managing Expenses: Working internationally, you have an amazing opportunity to save a lot of money by monitoring daily expenses and setting a budget. You are encouraged to see a financial advisor from your home country to set up a long-term budget plan that secures your financial future. Invest smartly. *See also our Budget, Expenses and Finances sections for more information.*

Markets: "Wet" markets, otherwise known as "public markets," derive their name from their wet floors from freshly-washed produce. Typically these are large, outdoor areas filled with individual stalls selling fresh produce, meats, seafood, herbs, spices and flowers. Arrive early in the morning for the best selection. These open air marketplaces offer an excellent opportunity not only to shop, but to experience the culture of your host country first hand. Keep in mind, most vendors accept cash only.

Marriage: In most cases marriages that are legally performed and valid abroad are also legitimate in your home country. Your embassy or a tourist information center in your host country will be your best source of information about marriage and legal processes involved. You may also need your consulate to authenticate your marriage document.

Measurements: Different regions use either metric or imperial measurement systems. Most commonly you might need to adapt in such areas as distance, weight and temperature. *See also our section on Clothing Sizes.*

Metric and US/Imperial Conversion Chart

- **Distance**

Metric		US/Imperial
1 millimeter (mm)	1 mm	0.03937 inches
1 centimeter (cm)	10mm	0.3937 inches
1 metre (m)	100cm	1.0936 yards
1 kilometer	1000m	0.6214 miles
US/Imperial		Metric
1 inch [in]	1 in	2.54 cm
1 foot [ft]	12 in	0.3048 m
1 yard [yd]	3 ft	0.9144 m
1 mile	1760 yds	1.6093 km

- **Mass**

Metric		US/Imperial
1 milligram (mg)	1 mg	0.0154 grain
1 gram (g)	1,000 mg	0.0353 oz
1 kilogram (kg)	1,000 g	2.2046 lb
US/Imperial		Metric
1 ounce (oz)	437.5 grain	28.35 g
1 pound (lb)	16 oz	0.4536 kg
1 stone	14 lb	6.3503 kg

- **Volume**

Metric		US/Imperial	
1 cu cm	1 cu cm	0.0610 in^3	
1 cu metre [m^3]	1,000 dm^3	1.3080 yd^3	
1 litre	1 dm^3	2.113 fluid	1.7598 pt
US/Imperial		Metric	
1 fluid ounce	1.0408 UK fl oz	29.574 ml	
1 pint (16 fl oz)	0.8327 UK pt	0.4732 liters	
1 gallon (231 in^3)	0.8327 UK gal	3.7854 liters	

- **Temperature**

  - To convert from Celsius to Fahrenheit, first multiply by 9/5, then add 32.
  - To convert from Fahrenheit to Celsius, first subtract 32, then multiply by 5/9.

Meeting New People: There are many ways to meet new people while living overseas. With that, most international schools provide opportunities for numerous social events. Also, get involved in local expat chapters and social groups.

Medical Records: Make certain you have copies of all your medical records. These should be kept in a safe place and be with you during all of your travels. Keep digital copies and leave a copy with a family member or close friend back home.

Medicines: If you must bring medications from home, be sure you have the accompanying letter/prescription and the medicine stored in the original container. In some cases prescriptions will need to be attested. Research your host country's laws and restrictions regarding bringing any prescription or non-prescription medicine into the country.

Money: Your contract will identify the currency in which you will be paid. If you are paid in local currency, it is essential that you understand that each currency value fluctuates independently. The value of your salary paid in local currency may not change at the same rate of your home country's currency. Your local bank can provide up-to-date conversion rates. In some countries the local currency is tied to the US dollar. *See Budget, Cash, Converting Cash, Expenses, Managing Expenses and Taxes sections for more information.*

Malaysia, Selayang, *Batu Caves*

-N-

Negotiations: Once a contract has been offered you have the right to negotiate; however, understand that most reputable international schools have very clear salary structures and criteria for appointment. As with all industries, be careful that your negotiation process does not leave a poor impression about what is important to you as a professional.

Newspapers: There are international English newspapers in most areas. You can also find a wide range available online.

GREAT IDEA: Seek out international and local newspapers to become more aware of local and regional events to better connect with your international student clientele.

Non-Government Organization (NGO): NGO's are legally constituted organizations created independently from any government. These organizations are often involved in charities, service and advocacy. Schools and teachers may choose to connect with NGO's for various humanitarian projects.

Non-Profit Schools: These are schools run by a board and driven by a clear mission to reinvest money into the quality of education or the community it serves.

Northern Hemisphere Schools: The school calendar years of northern and southern hemisphere schools are different. Just as the seasons fall at different times of the year around the world, school calendar years are influenced by these seasons. School years in the northern hemisphere usually begin in August/September after a long summer break.

Norway, Odda, *Trolltunga*

-O-

Occupations in International Schools: There are many other occupations available in international schools outside of teaching. If you have a non-teaching spouse/partner, consider:

- Admissions staff
- Security
- Business management
- Secretarial staff
- Finance staff
- Executive and administrative assistants
- Teacher aides
- Computer technicians
- Marketing/Promotions
- Custodial/Janitorial
- Human resources staff
- Purchasing staff
- Graphic arts
- Librarian assistant
- Translators
- Etc.

Offer of Contract: In the international community a verbal agreement is binding. Once offered a position ask for a 48-hour window to weigh your options and decide if the school is a good fit for you. Talk to your recruiting agent and study your contract. Discuss the job offer not only with your recruiting agent, but with family and friends. With that, you will get a range of different opinions - some informed and some not. This is all healthy to ensure you think critically and genuinely about a very important decision.   All of these factors will help you make an informed decision.

Organize: Organize your resources so that you are able to locate what you want to find in an efficient manner. This is especially important when living in a foreign country.

Ottawa, Canada, *Top of Library of Parliament of Ottawa*

-P-

Parents: Parents of all school students are universally similar in many ways. They care about their children, they want their children to have a quality education and they want their children to succeed.

Parents are also the same universally as they will see their child's education through the lens of their own educational experiences, cultures and traditions. This similarity is also what may make these parents different from parents of your past students. Because their unique cultural experiences may be different from your own experiences, it is important that you listen and understand these differences. Balance parents' needs with providing a strong education based on your school's mission and philosophy.

> **GREAT IDEA: Understand your students' parents. While one parent may judge the quality of their child's education by how many hours of homework their child receives each day, others may equate a good education with a strong performing arts program.**

Passport Photos: Before you leave your home country, obtain at least a dozen passport size photos including a digital copy. You will find that some countries require these photos for things such as cell phone purchases, liquor licenses (consumption), opening a bank account, etc. We suggest you take care of this in your home country as you are then well prepared.

Past Teaching Practices: It is exciting to be in an environment where best teaching practices are shared; however, be careful that you are not the person that insists on doing things "the way they have always been done." Don't fall into the trap of using a teaching method simply because it has been used in the past. Base best practice methods on proven outcomes instead of repetition or familiarity.

Performance Review: Most international schools will implement performance review processes for all staff. These tend to be more intensive for new teachers during their probationary period. Be proactive and investigate the process as it is written in your contract and upon arrival. See this as an opportunity for professional growth. *See also our Evaluation Process section.*

Personal Items: To help ease your transition into your host country, bring a month's supply of your favorite personal items. These personal items may include a certain

brand of make-up, face lotion, shaving cream, perfume or cologne. *See also our Female Items section.*

Pets: Transferring your pet to a foreign country can be difficult and may be traumatic for you both. There may be substantial paperwork, vaccinations and other prerequisites involved that you must complete before leaving your home country. Be aware that it could be very costly to relocate your pet and it is most likely not going to be paid for by your school. Consider too that many regions will require pets to be quarantined, often for significant lengths of time. Before making the decision to travel with your pet, weigh all these factors carefully. Sometimes the best choice is leaving your pet with a trusted friend or family member.

Questions to ask regarding your pet:
- Are pets allowed in my housing?
- Do you know a company or agency that can help transfer my pet?
- Are pets popular in my host country?
- Is there a quarantine period for my pet?
- How much will it cost to relocate my pet?
- How much notice does the airline require?
- Are there any specific shots my pet needs before entering the country?

Photos: Most international schools will require a photo on your CV. This photo should be a professional head shot. Include this photo in all correspondence with schools. This strategy will help you connect more directly with the reader of your correspondence.

Plagiarism: High-quality international schools have clear standards and policies regarding the management of plagiarism. Although the issue of plagiarism is common in all countries, there will be different perspectives in the community based on cultures and contexts. This difference between the school culture and the community's culture can be a challenge for teachers. Educate both students and parents by communicating policies and procedures clearly, as well as identifying what plagiarism looks like. There are a number of services online that will assist you in identifying plagiarism in your students' work.

Portfolio: Teachers are encouraged to create a professional portfolio that demonstrates the full range of their skills, abilities and philosophies. Portfolios should also demonstrate technology skills.

Sample categories for your portfolio may include:

- Personal information (CV, cover letter, photos, degrees and transcripts)
- Past evaluations
- Sample assessment rubrics
- Sample communication to parents and community
- Student assessment data

A good recruiting agent can also provide you with assistance creating your digital portfolio.

GREAT IDEA: Put your portfolio on a disk or online.

Postal Services: Different countries will have different levels of reliability in regard to postal services. Procedures may also be different. For example, some countries may require addresses written in both English and the local language. It is important to understand your host country's postal rules and regulations. You can find this information online or by simply asking a local.

GREAT IDEA: Some schools may allow you to receive your mail at the school which is often more reliable and convenient.

Power of Attorney: A power of attorney will allow someone to act on your behalf while you are out of the country. This is helpful in emergencies but is also convenient if you need important matters taken care of on your behalf. Get legal advice before leaving your home country regarding power of attorney. *See our section on Wills.*

Pregnancy: Just as you would at home, build a good relationship with your doctor and make all the necessary arrangements as you normally would. You will have access to high-quality medical care and support during pregnancy in most countries.

You will need to investigate the following school and country specific matters:

- Am I allowed maternity leave?
- What are the legal and residency implications of having a child in my host country?
- Do I have access to high-quality prenatal care?
- Do I have choices regarding my child's delivery?
- Is pregnancy and childbirth covered in my medical insurance?
- Is my newborn child automatically covered under my medical insurance?

- To whom do I report the birth of my child for registry and citizenship purposes in my home country?
- Is paternity leave available?

Profit Schools: The term "profit schools" usually refers to commercial education environments. Many international schools are commercial and their aim is to balance a high-quality education with earning a profit.

Public Transport: Although public transport in your host country may seem complicated, it is worth investigating the benefits of an often reliable means of transportation. Local contacts can assist you in understanding timetables, reliability and safety.

Pisa, Italy, *Leaning Tower of Pisa*

-Q-

Qualifications: There are no set qualifications to teach internationally. Ideally, international schools want to hire high-quality teachers that are specialists in their area of expertise.   The background of international teachers will be varied but selection criteria will focus primarily on how well the teacher's profile matches the needs of the students in the school.

GREAT IDEA: Have your recruiting agent look over your CV to ensure that your qualifications and experience are communicated in ways that best highlight your strengths for an international school environment.

Quarantine: Most countries have strict regulations within the customs process for items you want to bring into the country. Some items may be delayed during the quarantine processes so investigate guidelines before attempting to bring flora, fauna, food, pets and other items into a country. *See also our section on Pets.*

Queensland, Australia, *Great Barrier Reef*

-R-

Rate of Exchange: Be aware that conversion rates vary. Just because an agent offers "no fees" does not mean you are getting a great deal. The agent through whom you obtain money will receive commission either directly through fees or indirectly through an inflated conversion rate.

Recruiting Agent(s): Your recruiting agent will be your most valuable resource throughout the application and relocation processes. Seek out an agent who you can trust. The characteristics of a good recruiting agent are:

- ✓ Previous administration experience in international schools
- ✓ Broad understanding of international schools and the nature of international schools work environment
- ✓ Established networks with international schools
- ✓ Strong sense of values and demonstrated integrity
- ✓ Highly-accessible and highly-professional service
- ✓ A "critical friend" to help you make informed decisions that are in your best interests
- ✓ On-going support after appointment

GREAT IDEA: Choose a recruiting agent/company who you can trust to help you through this exciting journey.

References: You may be asked to provide professional and personal references. It is essential that your referees know what skills are important to international schools so they know which of your skills to showcase. It may be helpful to explain to your referees that discussing your capacity to meet the needs of children from different cultures, your use of differentiation and your ability to adapt to different ideas, teaching philosophies and cultures is essential.

Some schools will ask for references from up to three referees. If you are a new teacher, this would mean your college instructors might be good referees as well as your supervising teacher and other part-time work supervisors. You may also want to consider supervisors of community service projects in which you have participated.

Religion: It is important that you develop an understanding and respect for different religions around the world. Some country's laws will be driven by religious views which may be different from your own. In some countries this will influence your curriculum

decisions and topics you cover in the classroom. You should carefully research this topic, as well as others, before deciding on a host country.

Relocation Expenses: Most schools will allow you to make your own travel arrangements and reimburse you upon arrival in your host country. Typically there will be guidelines regarding reimbursement, including economy-class seating, most direct route, etc. Follow these guidelines closely and keep original receipts. You may also be provided a small allowance to ship additional items that are important to you.

Renewing Contract: A school may choose to offer you an extension of your contract. This usually happens within six-months of the end of your contract. This allows both parties to access the recruitment process with full knowledge of vacancies and availabilities.

GREAT IDEA: Talk to your recruiting agent well before your school's deadline for extension or renewal of contracts. This will give you an idea about what jobs might be available and help you to make an informed decision about your next steps.

Reputable Schools: A good recruiting agent should be a specialist in this field and therefore able to provide you the most current information, statistics and informed advice. You can also gather information about different schools on your own from a range of websites and social and professional networks; however, be aware that reading one opinion may not reflect the thoughts of many.

Resources: In your preparations for moving, you will need to consider what teaching resources you have already gathered which are transportable. You will also need to consider the needs of the school, students and curriculum you will be teaching.

It is important to reflect on the items you need to set up a comfortable lifestyle in your host country. To keep shipping to a minimum, consider what you will bring versus what you can acquire upon arrival. *See also Baggage and Shipping.*

Retirement: Some schools will provide a pension/retirement plan. This should be clear in your contract. If they do not offer a plan, consider this an important part of your budget process. It is also recommended that you see a financial planner in your home country to ensure your long-term financial goals are met.

Questions to ask regarding a retirement/pension plan:

- Do I have a retirement/pension plan?
- What are the contributions made by the school? By me?
- Do I have the option of making extra contributions?
- Is it easily transferrable when I end my contract?
- Is it compulsory?
- Do I have choices over the plan?

Red Square, Moscow, Russia, *St. Basil's Cathedral*

-S-

Safety: No matter what country you are living or working in, there are things you can (and should) do to ensure your safety:

- Travel lightly so you are less likely to set your luggage down.
- Buy a small safe for your home in your host country.
- Have a money belt that fits secretly under your clothing.
- Bring traveler's checks. Give a friend or family member a copy of serial numbers.
- Bring an extra set of passport photos along with an extra copy of your passport information page.
- Label each piece of luggage with your name, address, email address and phone number. Also put a copy of this information inside your luggage.
- Leave a copy of your itinerary and your passport with family and friends.
- Investigate local laws and customs of your host country and of countries you will be traveling.
- Stay in well-lit, high-traffic areas.
- Make a note of credit limits on your credit cards. Do not exceed those limits.
- Do not travel alone at night.
- Do not discuss travel plans or other personal matters with strangers.
- Do not talk to strangers who approach you.
- Beware of pickpockets and groups of vagrant children.
- Wear your handbag or satchel across your shoulder away from the curbside of your body to avoid "drive-by thieves."
- Walk with purpose. Only ask directions from people with authority.
- Learn a few emergency phrases or have them written down in case necessary.
- Only take taxis clearly identified with markings and a meter.
- Do not carry large amounts of cash.

GREAT IDEA: Even if you get rattled, demonstrate confidence. A confident person is less likely to be taken advantage of.

Salary: In reality there is no "average" or hard and fast rule as to what to expect regarding salary. Salaries vary depending on the school, country and other considerations. Salaries may range from $35,000 - $65,000 USD and many locations offer that tax free. You also need to consider the total value of your package inclusions, i.e., accommodations, medical insurance, pension, transport and other package allowances. In some countries you may be able to save up to two-thirds of your salary.

Savings: A good recruiting agent can help you predict your savings but ultimately it will depend on your lifestyle choices. A teacher living modestly can easily save two-thirds of his/her salary in some countries. Alternatively, you might choose location and lifestyle over savings. For example, living and working in Paris may offer you less in savings but afford you a great lifestyle while you are there.

School Management: The structures of school management and the terms used to describe leadership positions in international schools may be different than in your home country. Investigate not only your own job description, but understand the organizational structure, including reporting relationships, at your new school.

Setting Up Your Home: Many international environments have a high turnover of expatriates who will want to their sell household goods rather than pay to transport them to their new location. Check with teachers in your area to find these great deals on used furniture and supplies. It is common practice for people to buy things via notice boards, online advertising and garage sales. Use your network of new friends to find the best deals.

Shipping: Transport costs vary considerably depending on the speed of transfer. Research different shipping companies to find the most secure and cost-effective means of transport. Think carefully about what is necessary to bring compared to what you can buy when you arrive in your host country. *See also our Baggage section.*

Shopping: In your host country shopping may look different, you may pay with a different currency and you may have different product choices, but in all parts of the world it is an exchange of money for goods and services. Upon arrival, take a trip to your local shopping centers/markets and just browse the aisles. You will be surprised what familiar products will be available to you. Take your time paying in a new currency. Don't get flustered and shop around for best prices.

Shortage of International Teachers: Privatization of education is increasing rapidly all over the world. There is also an increased demand for international schools because parents want a high-quality education that prepares their children for a global world. Teachers with the skill set to match these needs are difficult to find due to reasons ranging from a lack of mobility to a lack of international-mindedness. If you are ready for an international experience, a good recruiting agent can help match your profile with the needs of an international school.

Sick Leave: Most schools allow at least five sick days a year; however, this will be dependent on the labor laws of your host country and individual school policies.

Sightseeing: One of the great things about teaching internationally is that there are new, amazing things to experience all over the world. Living in another country allows opportunities for sightseeing daily! Enjoy yourself and see the world.

Southern Hemisphere Schools: The school calendar years of northern and southern hemisphere schools are different. Just as the seasons fall at different times of the year around the world, school calendar years are influenced by these seasons. School years in the southern hemisphere usually begin in January after summer break.

Spouse: Some international schools have the resources to assist your non-teaching spouse in finding employment through partnership companies. If your spouse is interested in substitute teaching or providing daycare for working teachers, this is something that should be mentioned during your interview. *See also our section on Occupations in International Schools.*

Note: Teaching couples/partners are in high demand. Most recruiting agencies will have teaching couples complete a joint application and interviews may be done simultaneously.

Storage: Some international teachers choose to keep a storage unit in their home country and store the things that would be impossible to replace. One way to decide what should be stored is to balance the cost of the storage unit versus how long you will be overseas. It may be more cost effective to save the money from the larger storage unit and buy things new upon your return home. *See our section on Keys.*

> **GREAT IDEA: Create a list and take photos of items in your storage unit. This can be important for insurance purposes.**

Students: Some students will come to you academically prepared for "Ivy League" education from an early age. Other students will come from traditional education backgrounds and will need to adapt. It is important that you understand the differences and make sure you prepare all children equally.   Most students who attend international schools do so with the idea they will be fully prepared and competitive for the finest universities in the world. All international teachers are expected to teach to this belief.

Substitute Teaching: Even though teacher absence rates at international schools are often low, substitute teachers can be difficult to find. If your non-working partner is interested in casual, substitute employment, mention this during your interview.

Summer Break (Northern Hemisphere): Most international teachers use this extended break to travel home while making side trips to other travel destinations. Plan ahead of time and make the most of your travel allowance. Some summer breaks can be up to 10-weeks.

Support: International schools and expatriate environments create tight-knit social networks that serve as a great support system. In addition to this, maintain regular contact with the people that are important to you from home. Share your travels, schedule regular phone calls (VoIP is a great tool) and update social networks regularly. Remember: Good recruiting agents do not end their relationship with you once you have signed your contract. They will offer you support throughout your appointment.

Sao Paulo, Brazil, *Octavio Frias de Oliveira Bridge*

-T-

Taxes: Tax laws can be complicated in all countries. Your school may pay local taxes on your behalf or you may be responsible. While at home, investigate how income earned in another country should be handled.

Teaching Partners: Be clear at the interview if you have a partner or friend with whom you want to travel. Schools may often be more interested in teaching couples/partners because they are perceived to be a longer-term employment prospect. Because schools sometimes require you to share accommodations, it can also be cost effective for the school to hire teaching partners.

> **GREAT IDEA: If a housing allowance is provided, sharing accommodations with a friend can help maximize your savings.**

Technology and Integration: Best practice in international education is to use technology in an integrated model that maximizes student-learning outcomes. Most international schools offer innovative technology and expect teachers to integrate it into classroom practice.   Investigate what technology your new school uses and come well prepared with the skills and resources you need to adapt.

Television: Larger international cities have satellite television with international channels. If you are in a smaller city, you can check for online webcasts and video streaming programs.   These programs may require you to have a subscription and/or VPN to access video-streaming television.

Time Zones: As simple as it may sound, this can be stressful and frustrating both for you and your family and friends back home. It may be helpful to create a chart of what time it is in your host country compared to their time zone(s). There are many websites available to assist you.

> **GREAT IDEA: A great gift idea for your family and friends is a clock set at your host country's time. This will ensure they always know your local time.**

Traditions: Locals will value and appreciate your extra efforts to understand their traditions and cultures.

Ideas to enjoy and embrace your new community:

- Join the festivals
- Eat the food
- Exchange customary gifts
- Learn key phrases to celebrate the different holidays
- Ask questions and show interest
- Dress in traditional costumes (as appropriate)

Transformers: A transformer converts the voltage of appliances from different countries. For example, American appliances are 120-volts and many other countries use 220-240-volt appliances. Where possible, buy appliances in your host country. *See our sections on Adapters, Converters and Voltage.*

Translation Assistance: Often schools will provide basic translation assistance, but in time you may want to become more independent. Phrase books and smartphone and computer applications can assist you with translations. Please note that teachers in international environments rarely need to speak or understand the host country's language.

Transportation: Most schools provide transport to and from school. Other times you will have to pay for this at your own expense. Ask your school contact about taxi fees, subways and the city bus system.

> **GREAT IDEA:**   Travel like a local! Not only will it be cheaper, but you will see your new community in a different way.

Travel Opportunities: When you consider a location for employment, consider accessibility to large international airports. Living in a travel hub can provide significant advantages for travel opportunities as well as making it easier for flights home. Alternatively, regional areas can provide greater culture experiences, greater saving opportunities and easy access to travel hubs.

International teaching provides great opportunities for seeing different parts of the world both while you work and during breaks.

Trouble: If you need assistance unexpectedly, there are a range of contacts and support people who can help you. Your local consulate/embassy, your school and your

recruiting agent should be the first people you call to connect you with any support services you may need.

Thailand, Ayutthaya, *Sanphet Prasat Palace*

-U-

Used: Learn to love this word! Used furniture, household furnishings, books and many items will save you money, time and hassles. Many international environments have a high turnover of expatriates who will want to their sell household goods rather than pay to transport them. Check with teachers in your area to find these great deals on used furniture and supplies. It is common practice for people to buy things via notice boards, online advertising and garage sales. Use your network of new friends to find the best deals.

Utilities: Most schools cover or contribute to your cost of utilities. If you are responsible for utilities, investigate what the average expenses will be at different times of the year.

Ukraine, Yalta, *Swallow's Nest*

-V-

Vacancies: Most reputable international schools work through recruitment agencies. A good recruiting agency will provide access to a database of teaching vacancies around the world. Although vacancies may open at various times throughout the school year, you will need to begin your application process six to twelve months prior to your planned departure date.

> **GREAT IDEA: Be open-minded about the regions you are considering. Commonly, teachers find great opportunities in areas that they had not previously considered.**

Vaccinations: All countries have different vaccination requirements. It will be your responsibility to investigate your host country's requirements. Travel websites and government websites often provide thorough details about required vaccinations. Your recruiting agent can also help you find this information.

Visa Procedures: Most schools will start your visa process as soon as you sign your contract. This can be a slow process depending on the country so it is important that you obtain all requested information and submit by the scheduled deadlines. Missing a visa deadline could delay your arrival into your host country.

Make sure there is at least six months before your passport expires. Also, make sure you have plenty of blank pages for visa stamps and work permits.

Although not all countries' visa procedures are the same, there are many things that you will find consistent. Some documents that may be requested from you:
- ✓ Copy of passport
- ✓ Resume
- ✓ Copy of your birth certificate
- ✓ Copy of diplomas/certificates (high school and university)
- ✓ Copy of teaching qualification(s)
- ✓ Copy of dependents' passports (if applicable)
- ✓ Copy of marriage certificate (if applicable)
- ✓ Copy of child's birth certificate (if applicable)
- ✓ "Proof of work" letter: Some countries require a letter from your previous employer(s) that certifies your occupation, area of work, length of

employment and job description. This letter should be written on company letterhead and signed by your employer.

- ✓ You may also be asked to provide the following information:
- ✓ Place of birth (including country, state and city)
- ✓ Current address
- ✓ Permanent address (including apartment number if applicable, street, city, state, country and postal code)
- ✓ Permanent contact number
- ✓ Emergency contact person
- ✓ Contact details of emergency contact person
- ✓ Digital passport size photo

Be aware: Do not accept employment that requires you to enter your host country on a visitors' or tourist visa. Although some times this may be acceptable, in many cases you are putting yourself at risk of violating your host country's labor laws.

Visitors: Check with your school and ask if they have accommodations available for your visiting family and friends. Sometimes you will have plenty of space in your own accommodations, but otherwise your school may be able to recommend local hotels that offer discounted rates. *See our section on Guests.*

GREAT IDEA: Have an extra cell phone with reliable contacts for visitors to access. Also provide visitors with maps and directions.

Vocational Training: Most international schools have a clear academic pathway; however, some are now moving into vocational programs. If you have particular skills in this area, include them in your application and talk to your recruiting agent.

Voltage: Voltage varies in different regions of the world. Most appliances can tolerate some variance in voltage; however, severe variations can damage electrical equipment. If you are bringing an appliance from home, check that the variance is within reasonable limits. With that, the safest plan is to buy appliances in your host country. *See also our section on Adaptors, Convertors and Transformers.*

Some Common Voltages:

Australia - 240 V	China - 220 V	Spain - 230 V
Bahamas - 120 V	Finland - 230 V	United Kingdom - 230 V
Brazil - 120/220 V	Japan - 100 V	United States - 120 V
Canada - 120 V	Mexico - 127 V	Vietnam - 127/220 V

Voting: Your home country is likely to have a process that allows citizens living outside of their country to vote in local, state and national elections. Investigate your eligibility and the process as it applies to you.

VPN (Virtual Private Network) Accounts: A VPN account is a private network account that creates a virtual connection through the Internet to connect you to a remote site. This is commonly used by people who want to access a wider and less restrictive range of internet sites than their region allows. VPN accounts can be purchased online. *See our Internet section.*

Venice, Italy, *Grand Canal*

-W-

Weekends: Some schools may require you to lead some extracurricular activities, excursions, camps or professional development on weekends. Some of these activities may be a part of your contract while others may involve a small stipend. You may also work for a school that administers student testing on Saturdays. Otherwise, weekends are your own to explore, sightsee and rest.

GREAT IDEA: Find out when the weekend is! In some countries the weekend is Friday and Saturday and you are back to work on Sunday!

Weighing Your Options: When offered a position, it is important to consider some key factors:

Salary: Consider not only how much you are being paid, but how much of your salary is potential savings. For example, many international schools pay 100% of housing and utilities. This and other package inclusions are important to consider when comparing "bottom line" figures.

Remember, in your home country you may have a higher gross salary, but taxes, housing, transportation and utilities could eat up a large part of your savings. Also, the chance to see the world and experience different cultures is priceless!

Lifestyle: What will your lifestyle look like in the short term as well as the long term based on this decision?

Travel: Are you interested in seeing the world? Do you want to see the world now or after you retire? Working internationally affords you the opportunity to teach where you travel. Because international schools recognize teachers' mobility, most contracts are signed for a two-year period with an option to renew after that time. This allows you to immerse yourself in different cultures and travel to different parts of the world.

Professional Opportunities: There are world-renowned schools in many different parts of the world that exclusively hire international teachers. These opportunities provide you with a skill set and experiences that may or may not be available in your home country.

Benefits: Most international schools provide an annual round-trip airfare to your home country, full worldwide medical coverage, housing, utilities, professional development (sometimes this involves traveling to different parts of the world) and competitive salaries.

Working towards your next job: Identify opportunities within your school to expand your skill set. Some international schools do not require certification in leadership to become a principal/headmaster. Directors of international schools are looking for proven abilities and demonstrated outcomes for leadership, counseling, librarian and head teaching opportunities.

If you are looking for career advancement, you will have opportunities to work in new areas. International schools are always looking for ways to push the boundaries on best practices.

Wills: Seek legal counsel from an attorney before leaving your home country in regards to the creation of a well-written will. *See our section on Power of Attorney.*

Winter Break (Northern Hemisphere): Each school will create a calendar that reflects the needs of the curriculum and the holidays of the host country. In some cases the school will recognize holidays from different countries depending on affiliations with that country and/or the curriculum it represents. In most cases the school calendar will represent the holidays of the host country. Note that these holidays may or may not reflect your own religious traditions or customs.

Washington, D.C., United States of America, *Capitol Building*

-X-

Xenophobia: Some people have an irrational fear of other cultures, countries and people. As an international teacher living and working in another country, you have the opportunity to influence and build new cultural bridges between your home country and many other cultures of the world. Share stories, educate others and help build a more globally-minded world.

Xi'an, China, *Terracotta Warriors*

-Y-

Yearly Reflection: Once a year, take the time to reflect both professionally and personally on your growth and adventures. Make the most of this opportunity.

Things to consider:

- Professional
- Am I stretching myself?
- What have I learned?
- Am I motivated and satisfied in my current position?
- What are my strengths?
- What are my areas of improvement?
- Where do I see myself in 5 years?
- What am I doing on a daily basis that contributes to my school? My community?
- What actions and behaviors demonstrate my international-mindedness?

Personal:

- Is my life balanced?
- Am I making the most of this opportunity through travel, experiences, relationships, etc.
- Am I working toward my financial goals?
- Am I living a healthy lifestyle?
- Am I documenting and sharing this journey through pictures, journals, etc.?

Yerevan, Armenia, *church*

-Z-

Zzzz…

Take a rest! Teaching internationally is an important life-changing decision to be made in partnership with your family, friends and your recruiting agent. Reflect and embrace the exciting opportunities that lie ahead.

> **GREAT IDEA: Create a scrapbook and begin collecting memories of your new adventure.**

We have given you a lot of information but don't let it overwhelm you. Take one step at a time and depend on those around you for guidance and support. Now that you have this information available to you, you can make an informed decision that we know will be one of the most exciting decisions of your life.

We wrote this book because we have experienced first-hand the wonderful opportunities that working internationally can provide. We look forward to providing you with advice, support and assistance.

Best wishes and safe travels!

Zanzibar, *Zanzibar Beach*

Other Titles by Shanna Mack and Greg Parry

Congratulations! You've been invited to interview. Now what?

There are dozens, if not hundreds, of books out there offering advice on how to land "a job. " But teaching is not just "a job" and the interview process is unlike any other. Books that coach you to memorize pithy answers or "play a role" will not serve you well if you want to land a quality position with a well-respected school.

A+ Interviewing for Educators is not just a laundry list of questions and canned responses, but a thoughtful plan-of-action, written by two highly-qualified educators who have sat on both sides of the interview table. Because of their unique combination of experience, the authors are able to offer a glimpse into the interviewers' psyche helping you prepare not just "good" responses, but an understanding of what he/she is looking for. They also walk you through the interview process, including potential pitfalls as well as opportunities to shine. Areas covered include: personal philosophy, dealing with parents, leadership style, student engagement, special needs students and dealing with stress.

If you're serious about teaching, this is the *one book* that will help you land that dream job. And, for those who are considering international opportunities, there's a special section dedicated to that unique situation.

Packed with insider tips and expert advice, *A+ Interviewing for Educators* is the single best way to ensure walking into that next interview with confidence, prepared to accept an offer!

Available online at www.GlobalServicesInEducation.com